LIFE IN THE
MOUNTAINS

Written by **Catherine Bradley**

Consultant Roger Hammond
Director of Living Earth

First published in Great Britain in 1991 by
Two-Can Publishing Ltd
346 Old Street, London EC1V 9NQ

Copyright © Two-Can Publishing Ltd, 1991
Text copyright © Catherine Bradley, 1991
Design by Belinda Webster

Printed in Hong Kong by Wing King Tong Co. Ltd.

The JUMP! logo and the word JUMP!
are registered trade marks.

British Library Cataloguing in Publication Data
Bradley, Catherine
Life in the mountains
1. Mountainous regions
I. Title
909.09430829
ISBN: 1-85434-141-3

Photographic Credits:
p.4-5 Bruce Coleman/Dieter & Mary Plage p.7 (top) Bruce Coleman/Steve Kaufman (bottom) Bruce Coleman/C.B. & D.W. Frith p.8 (left) ZEFA/Ned Gillette (centre) London/Ian Beames p.9 (right) Bruce Coleman/Stephen J. Krasemann p.10 (bottom left) Ardea, London/François Gohier (top right) Ardea, London/Kenneth W. Fink (right) Bruce Coleman/Hans Reinhard (bottom right) Survival Anglia/Clive Huggins p.12 Survival Anglia/Jeff Foott p.13 (top) Bruce Coleman/Erwin and Peggy Bauer (bottom) Bruce Coleman/Steve Kaufman p.14 Bruce Coleman/C.B. & D.W. Frith p.15 (top) Survival Anglia/Richard & Julia Kemp (bottom left) Ardea, London/Eric Dragesco (bottom) Ardea, London/Kenneth W. Fink p.16 (top) Hutchison Library p.17 Ardea, London/Richard Waller p.18 (bottom left) Ardea, London/S. Roberts (right) Hutchison Library/ZEFA p.20 Bruce Coleman/Hans Reinhard p.21 Bruce Coleman/Dieter & Mary Plage p.22 Bruce Coleman/Gerald Cubitt p.22 Bruce Coleman/M.P. Price

Front cover: Bruce Coleman/Wayne Lankinen. Back cover: Ardea, London/Eric Lindgren.

Illustrations by Michaela Stewart. Story written by Claire Watts. Edited by Monica Byles.

CONTENTS

All words marked in **bold** can be found in the glossary

LOOKING AT MOUNTAINS

High above the valleys and plains soar the mighty mountains of the world. Mountains come in many different shapes and sizes. They can be jagged, icy peaks, smoking **volcanoes**, or even green and fertile islands.

A wide and unique variety of animals, plants and people have adapted to life on the steep and rocky slopes. Some insects also live on the mountain pastures. A few, like glacier fleas, can even live in ice and snow.

THE HEART OF THE EARTH

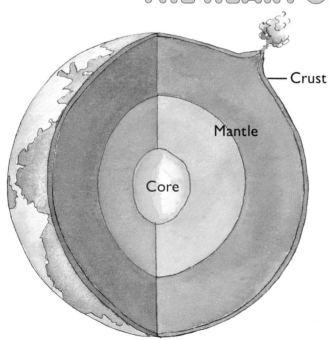

— Crust

Mantle

Core

The Earth is like an onion, made up of different layers of rock. The centre, or **core**, of the Earth is likely to be made of nickel and iron. The next layer outwards is the **mantle**, a tightly packed band of rock about 3,000 km thick. We live on the cool, outermost layer, or **crust**. This is up to 50 km thick in most places.

Near the Earth's crust, the rocks of the mantle are hot and molten. This liquid rock is squeezed from every side. Where the crust is weak it spews out the rock or lava, and forms a type of mountain called a volcano.

Very few mountains rise alone from a plain. Usually they form part of a longer chain or range of mountains, such as the Andes, which run the length of the west coast of South America. As the Earth's surface changes, new mountains form slowly, over millions of years, as older ones gradually wear away.

This book looks mainly at the many different forms of life on the mighty mountains of the world.

▼ Mount Everest in the Himalayas is the highest peak on Earth. It is 8,848 m high. The Himalayas are the world's most recently formed mountain range. It is 2,400 km long and 6,000 m high, on average.

MAKING MOUNTAINS

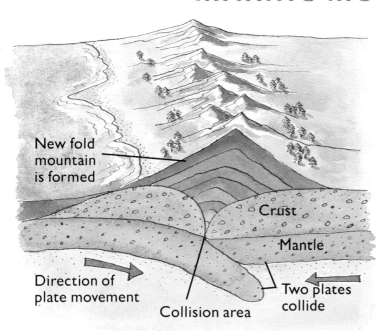

New fold mountain is formed

Crust

Mantle

Direction of plate movement

Two plates collide

Collision area

Large areas of the crust, called **plates**, move slowly around on the Earth's surface. The oceans and continents ride on the plates. Long ago, the plates were joined. Their edges could still fit together like pieces of a puzzle.

Sometimes the plates meet and grind together, causing earthquakes. At their edges the rocks slowly fold upwards to form **fold mountains**, or drift apart to form valleys.

One plate may make the edge of another plate sink, while the rocks at its own edge rise very slowly to make a new range of mountains.

WHERE IN THE WORLD?

Any land over 300 m above the surrounding flat land can be called mountainous. Mountains cover about one-fifth of the Earth's surface. The continents of Australia and Africa have only very few mountains, while Asia has huge areas of mountainous land across its surface.

Vast underwater mountains also form part of the floors of the oceans. Hawaii is the topmost part of an underwater volcano. Measured from the sea floor, it is even higher than Mount Everest at over 9,000 m tall.

Block mountains have broad, flat tops, or **plateaux**. These mountains form when blocks of rock are forced up through cracks, or faults, in the crust by the liquid rock in the mantle. Rift valleys form when rock slides into a crack in the crust.

▼ This map shows the main mountain ranges. The younger ones, the Alps, the Rockies, the Andes and the Himalayas, are fold mountains. The Scottish Highlands, the Atlas and Appalachian Mountains, the Drakensberg, the Urals and the Pyrenees are older and have been worn by the weather for millions of years.

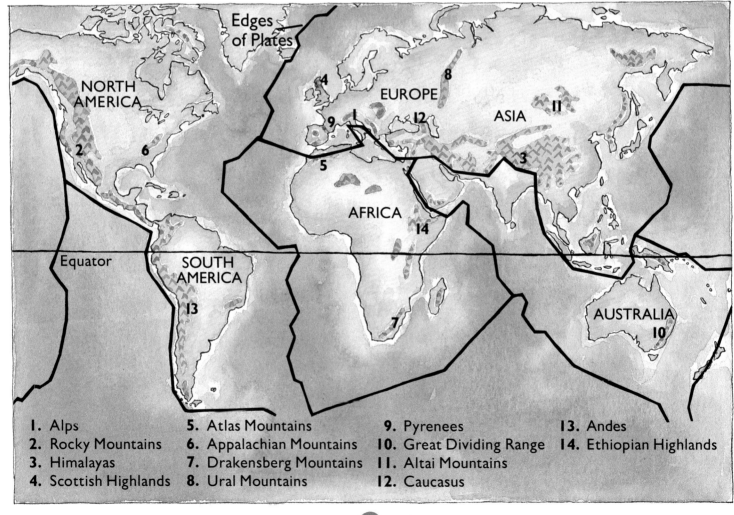

1. Alps	5. Atlas Mountains	9. Pyrenees	13. Andes
2. Rocky Mountains	6. Appalachian Mountains	10. Great Dividing Range	14. Ethiopian Highlands
3. Himalayas	7. Drakensberg Mountains	11. Altai Mountains	
4. Scottish Highlands	8. Ural Mountains	12. Caucasus	

◀ Mount Augustine is a live volcanic island off the coast of Alaska, USA. In 1986, it erupted and ash and gases spouted from its crater.

▼ Weird limestone mountains stand near the Guilin Li River in China. Limestone is soft and is gradually worn away by the wind, or dissolved by rain. Over the years, these unusual mountains have been slowly ground into strange shapes.

ICE, SNOW AND RAIN

Mountains change all the time. Over the years, heavy rains soften their rocky outlines, and gather to form rivers. These eventually carve deep V-shaped channels or valleys into the side of the mountain.

Ice and snow also change the shape of the mountains. There is less air high up a mountain to trap the warmth of the Sun's rays. It is very cold and many of the world's peaks are covered with a deep blanket of snow and ice throughout the entire year.

RAIN SHADOWS

Rain-filled clouds blow towards the land from the sea. They release their moisture when they reach cold mountain air. The landward side of a mountain receives little rain and is called the **rain shadow**.

▲ Sometimes snow gets too heavy and slips down the mountainside as an **avalanche**.

▶ Ice may form slow-moving rivers called glaciers. Stones and rocks in the ice **erode,** or wear away, the mountains, leaving U-shaped channels, known as glaciated valleys. The glacier melts as it gets further from the cold peak and into warmer areas. This is the John Hopkins glacier in Alaska, USA.

▼ Heavy rains often loosen the earth on a mountain and lead to a landslide. Strong winds may also blow away rocks and soil and change its shape. Sometimes heavy rocks and earth tumble down a mountainside damaging buildings and injuring people.

TREES AND PLANTS

At high **altitudes**, it becomes harder for mountain plants to survive the cold and lack of water. Completely different plants will grow on a protected sunny slope than on a slope exposed to icy winds.

In the northern hemisphere, both **deciduous** and **coniferous** trees grow on the lower slopes. Further up, the deciduous trees thin out, and the conifers grow more thickly. Beyond, a few conifers struggle to the **treeline**. Above this, conditions are too harsh for trees to grow. The height of the treeline varies with **latitude** and local weather patterns. Mountains away from the **Equator** are colder and have lower treelines.

In tropical areas, dense rainforests grow lower down, while lush 'cloud' forests of mossy **evergreens** grow further up the mountain slopes.

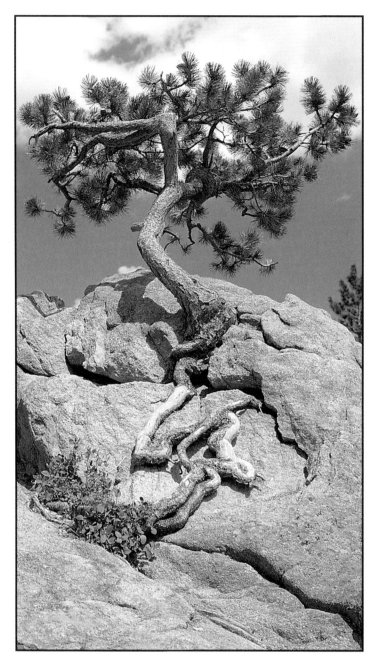

▲ A small Ponderosa pine anchors itself in a boulder on a steep mountainside. The waxy needle-like leaves contain very little water to freeze, and are shaped so that most snow will slide off the branches and not harm the tree.

◀ Cushions of grass, moss and lichen grow on the thin soil and rock of the upper slopes. At ground level they are sheltered from the winds. All plant life stops at the **snowline**.

► In summer, the meadows high up in the European Alps are covered in a rich carpet of flowers. The plants must be sturdy to combat the cold and windy conditions. They are only a few centimetres high and have stems that can bend in the wind. Their roots hold them firmly in place. The petals are brightly coloured to attract the few insects living there.

PLANT PANEL

In the northern hemisphere, deciduous and coniferous trees grow on the lower slopes. Higher up, only coniferous trees survive. Once past the treeline, shrubs, grasses and flowers may grow on the thin mountain soil.

▼ The giant lobelia lives on Mount Kenya. It traps air in its hairs to keep warm. It grows up to 8m tall and has spiky blue flowers.

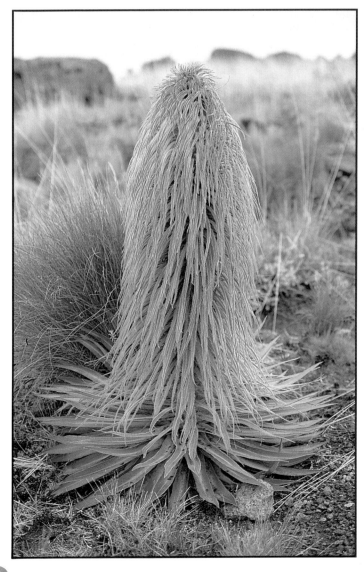

KEEPING WARM

Mountain animals have long hair with a thick undercoat of fur to keep them warm. They are often larger than relatives in valleys and plains. Some animals, like wild sheep and goats, feed on the top pastures in summer, and move downhill in winter. Smaller animals, like Alpine marmots and the mountain hares of Europe and Asia, feed mainly in the top meadows. Marmots feed all summer, then **hibernate** for eight months of the year and lose as much as one-quarter of their body fat.

Several **predators** stalk the mountains. In the Himalayas, rare snow leopards live near the snowline and prey on grazing animals. In Europe, hunters like wolves and lynxes are occasionally seen.

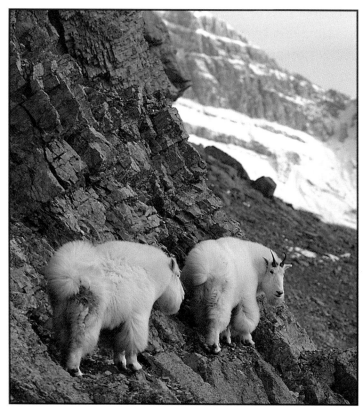

▲ Mountain goats have hard, sharp hooves which grip the rock like pincers as they move about the slippery top slopes to graze.

ANIMAL FACTS

● Pikas are found on European, Asian and North American mountains. They feed on grasses and other plants. They spend the summer building up stores of food to eat during the winter.

● The snow rabbit and the mountain hare both turn white in the winter so that they are hidden against the snow. This form of protection against predators is called **camouflage**.

► The North American cougar lives close to the snowline during the summer. Cougars, like brown bears and lynxes, prey on goats and other grazing animals.

▼ The macaque monkeys in the Shiga Highlands of Japan have learned to keep warm in the local hot springs. They cook their vegetables in the hot water before eating them. Here, one monkey checks fur for ticks and fleas.

FLYING AND HOPPING

Animals living on either side of a mountain range are often quite unrelated. Some birds and insects, however, manage to overcome the altitude and cross the mountains. Birds must have thick feathers and efficient lungs to be able to fly so high. Specially equipped birds include the bar-headed geese, which migrate from Siberia to their distant wintering grounds in India.

The large birds of prey that live close to the mountain peaks include the giant Andean condor, the lammergeier and the golden eagle. There are also smaller birds that remain close to the ground, such as the Alpine chough in Europe and Asia, which feeds on insects, butterflies and mountain plants.

FLYING HIGH

The Apollo butterfly lives on some of the highest mountains of Europe and Asia. It flies only when sunshine warms it. When the Sun goes behind a cloud, it drops to the ground to save energy. The Apollo is now protected by law from keen butterfly collectors in most of its habitats in Europe.

◀ The mountain grasshopper has stiff flaps where its wings used to be. Those insects, like butterflies, that do still fly, stay near the ground so they do not get blown away by the wind. Some insects even survive above the snowline.

▶ In the French Pyrenees a male capercaillie struts about in the snow, searching for a mate. Its call is a series of crackles and pops. The capercaillie mainly feeds on buds, and cones. It is the largest type of grouse.

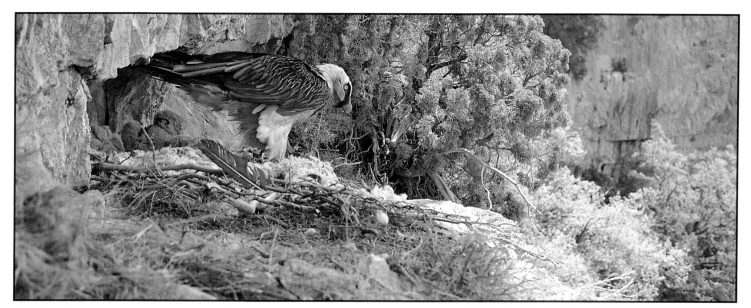

▲ The lammergeier nests in the peaks. It is a large mountain vulture native to Europe, Asia and Africa, and feeds mostly on dead animals. Most other birds could not survive in the cold.

▶ The hummingbirds of the high Andes become sluggish when it is cold at night. This is a red-tailed comet hummingbird.

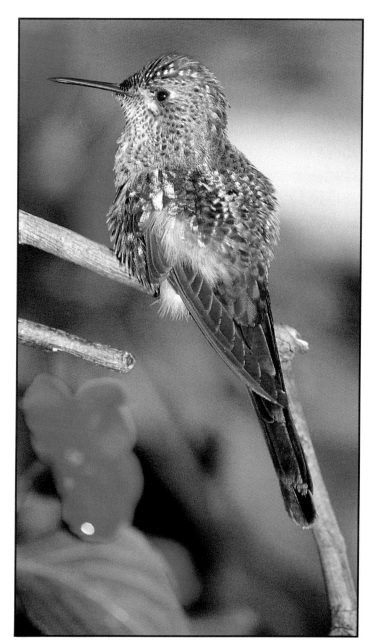

MOUNTAIN DWELLERS

Lowland people are exhausted at high altitudes. There is little oxygen and it is extremely cold. Mountain people have adapted to these harsh conditions. People like the Bhotia in the Himalayas have enlarged hearts and lungs and wide nostrils so that their bodies may take in enough oxygen. They depend on sturdy yaks, members of the cattle family, to provide them with meat, wool, milk, transport, hides, and butter.

In many areas, such as the Rocky Mountains, the European Alps, and Scandinavia, farmers rear dairy cattle and sheep in the mountains. The animals are often kept in barns on the valley floors to shelter from the winter snows, and in the summer are herded to the higher pastures to be fattened on the rich grasses.

▲ An Afghan woman dressed in richly coloured clothing milks her goat in the Hindu Kush.

► A lively market takes place in the Sherpa capital of Namche in Nepal. Sherpas farm, raise animals and trade. They often act as guides and porters for mountaineering expeditions.

PEOPLE FACTS

● The Lapps are nomads living in northern Sweden. Some Lapps keep reindeer to provide meat and milk, and skin to make tents and clothes.

● The Andean peoples of South America keep llamas, vicuñas and alpacas. Some mine tin, copper, gold and silver. Others grow barley and potatoes.

MOUNTAIN TREASURES

Valuable resources such as coal, metals like copper, zinc and iron ores, as well as semi-precious and precious minerals, are mined from mountains. The bare rock itself is used by the building industry.

The banks of the Rocky Mountains in Canada are covered with useful softwoods, like aspen, pine and spruce. Hardwoods like teak, ebony, mahogany and rosewood grow on tropical mountains. Ships, furniture and building materials are made from different types of wood.

Mountain rivers are often dammed to feed a reservoir of water. The rushing torrent turns huge turbines which generate enough electricity to power whole cities or even nations, such as mountainous Switzerland.

▼ A dam is built on Columbia River, Canada, to store water for the use of city-dwellers.

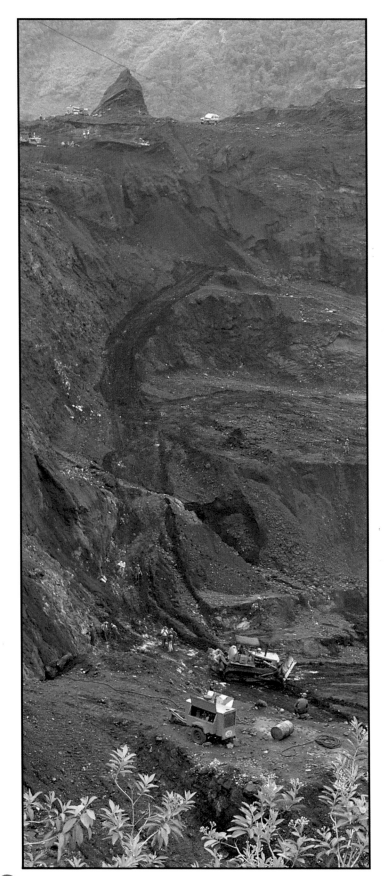

► A loader piles logs on to the back of a trailer. When trees are felled on mountain slopes, the rain is no longer absorbed by the roots but runs freely, washing soil into the rivers. In the end, the slopes are left bare and eroded. With proper management, wood can be cut from special plantations.

◄ Emeralds are mined in the Andes, in Colombia. The stones are cut and polished to make jewellery.

MOUNTAIN STOREHOUSE

Jewels, such as diamonds, rubies, emeralds, sapphires, quartz, gold and platinum are taken from minerals and rocks found in the mountains.

Granite and marble may be used in building banks, town halls or palaces. Slate is used for making roofing tiles, and limestone is used to make cement.

Copper, zinc and iron are extracted from mountain rocks. They are used in construction and sculpture, and to make jewellery, tools and utensils.

Softwoods are important for use in the construction of buildings, for making paper and as fuel. Hardwoods are used for making long-lasting furniture.

MOUNTAINS IN DANGER

There are many threats to the mountains. Summer visitors can erode paths and crush rare plants. New ski resorts may scar whole mountainsides with cable-cars and ski-lifts.

Everywhere, mountain forests are being damaged. In many industrial nations **acid rain** harms mountain forests. Cars and factories produce chemicals which **pollute** the rain. In Nepal, many trees are felled for fuel. Remaining tree roots cannot absorb enough rainwater, and so the fertile topsoil washes into the rivers, flooding them downstream. The mountain slopes are left bare, stripped down to their barren rock.

Mining can destroy a mountain, leaving only ugly waste. In Western Australia, entire mountains are dug away to remove their iron ore.

▲ In the Black Forest, southern Germany, mountain trees are poisoned by acid rain. The trees lose their leaves, wither and die.

▶ This rubbish was left by climbers on Mount Everest. Much of the rubbish is plastic, which will never break down, but will continue to blow around the mountainside for many years.

EROSION

Earthworms help to wear down the mountains. Air and rain travel down the tunnels to break down rocks below. Fragments of rock come to the surface in the wormcasts, and are washed away.

In 1900, forests covered 40 per cent of Ethiopia. Trees were felled, and crops and cattle eroded the bare earth. Today, trees cover only four per cent of mountainous Ethiopia and there are often famines.

SAVE THE MOUNTAINS

In many countries, people have completely changed the nature of their local mountains. In some areas of Greece, for example, the forests have been cut down, and sheep and goats have eaten the remaining vegetation. The mountains are reduced to bare rock as the unprotected soil has been completely eroded by wind and rain.

Some countries have created national parks to protect their mountains. Forests are managed so that when one tree is cut down, another is planted. The habitat of wild animals, plants and birds is protected from damage by people and industry. In this way, mountains can remain areas of great beauty.

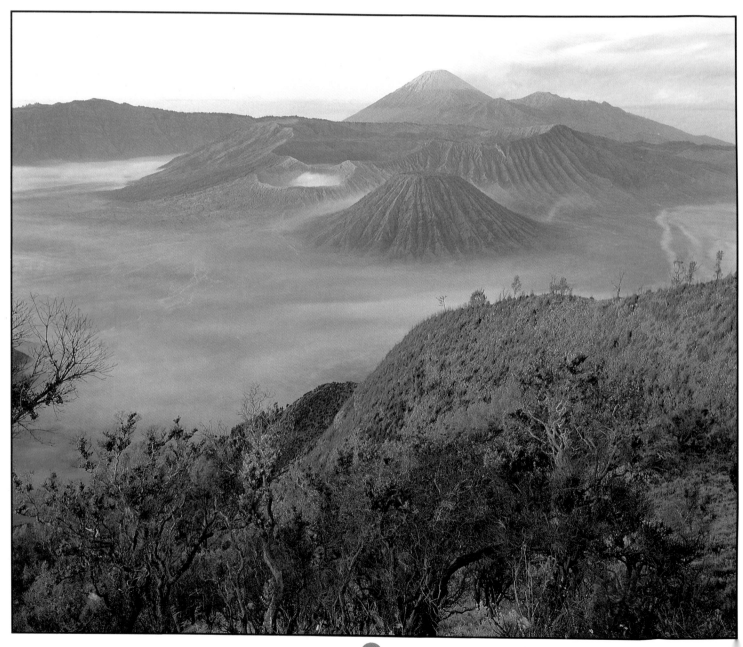

All the world's mountains should be protected against long-lasting damage from mining, logging, and the erosion that follows. Mountains play an important role in the Earth's weather patterns and support a unique variety of animals and plants.

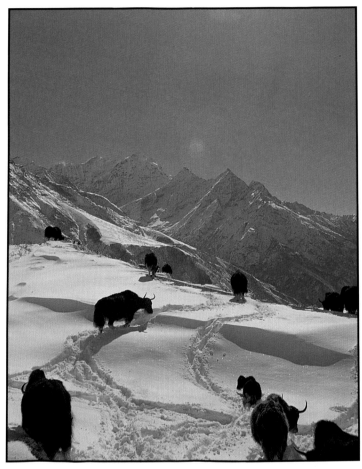

▲ The yak, or grunting ox, lives on the slopes of the Himalayas, in Nepal. These animals have long been used by local people for transport and as a supply of meat and milk. Local people must fight to preserve their traditional ways of life in the mountains.

◀ A volcano rises through the pearly dawn mist in East Java, Indonesia. New volcanoes are formed regularly along lines of faults in the Earth's crust, while old volcanoes cool and become extinct.

WHAT CAN YOU DO?

Support ecology campaigns:

● There are many groups which campaign to protect mountains and other endangered areas. Find out about their work in magazines and newspapers, on the radio or on television.

● Tell your friends and relatives about acid rain and mountains in danger.

● Write to the government and ask its ministers to fight to protect mountains and help prevent acid rain.

When you go walking or climbing in the mountains, follow some essential rules:

● Use only the signposted paths.

● Never pick wild flowers.

● Try not to tread on any plants growing on the mountainside.

HOW COYOTE STOLE FIRE

For thousands of years people have told stories about the world around them. Often these stories try to explain something that people do not understand, like how the world began. This story, told by North American Indians, tries to explain how fire was discovered at the top of a volcanic mountain.

Long ago, when the world was young, Coyote passed by the camp where the People lived. The midday sun was shining on the first snow of winter, and all the People were huddled together in their chilly teepees, far too cold to venture out into the world.

"If only we could keep just a little piece of the warm summer sun in our teepees in the winter," said one, wrapping his thick blanket around him more tightly against the draught. He sneezed and looked miserable.

Coyote pitied the People. His own fur grew thick and warm during the winter. Then Coyote had an idea. Perhaps he could help them!

Coyote travelled all the next day to the very top of a nearby mountain. There, in a huddle, sat three fiery creatures, guarding a tiny fire.

As Coyote approached, the three fiery creatures began to sniff the mountain air and look around them suspiciously. They chattered,

"Who's that? Who's trying to steal our fire? Go away!"

When they saw Coyote, the three fiery creatures began to hiss loudly. They stretched out their fiery fingers towards him until he was forced to back off. Then they settled down around the fire again.

But Coyote had not gone very far. He ran off a little way and then crept back and hid behind some bushes to keep watch.

The three fiery creatures spent the whole day guarding the fire but, as night began to fall, two of them disappeared into a nearby cave. A few hours later, the creature left by the fire went to the mouth of the cave and called out to the others.

The second creature soon came out to take his place. Later, the second creature went to the mouth of the cave and called out. This time there was no reply. He called again, but still got no answer. Finally, he went right inside the cave, and the fire was left unguarded for a few minutes before the third creature came out.

Coyote watched all this with interest. In fact, he sat watching the fiery creatures for three whole days and nights. Every day, the fire was guarded all the time, except for a few minutes of the night when all three fiery creatures went inside the cave. This was his one chance.

On the fourth night Coyote was ready. When the second fiery creature went into the cave to wake up the third, he ran towards the fire, picked up a flaming branch in his jaws and dashed off down the steep side of the mountain.

As he ran, he heard the sounds of screaming behind him. The fiery creatures had discovered their loss and were now chasing after him.

Coyote ran and ran, but the fiery creatures were much faster than him. At last, one of them came near enough to grab at Coyote's tail. He snatched at it with his fiery hand and scorched the tip of Coyote's tail white. To this day, all coyotes have a white tip to their tails.

When Coyote felt the fiery fingers on his tail, he tossed the flaming branch high into the air. Squirrel leapt down from a tree, grabbed the branch, and ran off down the mountain with it. The fiery creatures followed.

Still they ran too fast. Squirrel felt their burning breath on her back, singeing her fur. To this day, her tail curls up from the scorching heat.

Squirrel threw the branch to Chipmunk, who ran on down the mountain with the fiery creatures close behind.

It took only a few minutes before the fiery creatures began to gain on Chipmunk. He felt the fiery claw of one of them grab at his back, but wriggled away. And to this day, chipmunks have stripes down their backs from the fiery claw-marks.

Reaching the bottom of the mountain, Chipmunk threw the burning branch to Frog. Poor Frog could not run very fast at all. The fiery beings swept down on him and one of them grabbed him by the tail. But with one enormous leap, Frog jumped out of the creature's hand, leaving his tail behind. To this day, frogs have no tails.

As soon as he had put some distance between himself and the fiery creatures, Frog threw the flaming branch across to Wood, who swallowed it whole.

The fiery creatures did not know what to do. They were desperate and kicked and scratched and bit at Wood, but he refused to give back their fire. They sat near Wood for four whole days before giving up.

But Coyote knew how to get the fire out of Wood. He taught the People how to twist a stick between their hands with the pointed end rubbing a hole in a piece of wood until a spark appeared. Then the People learned to feed the spark with dry grass until they had a flame. The People could now warm themselves and would never need to be cold again.

TRUE OR FALSE?

Which of these facts are true and which ones are false? If you have read this book carefully, you will know the answers.

1. The outer layer of the Earth is called the mantle.

2. The Earth's plates once fitted together like a giant jigsaw puzzle.

3. Mountains cover about half of the Earth's surface.

4. Land on a mountainside facing away from the sea often receives very little rain.

5. Alpine flowers are often dull in colour to attract local insects.

6. Trees can only survive up to the treeline on the slopes of a mountain.

7. Marmots hibernate all year round and lose most of their body weight.

8. The macaque monkeys of Japan have learned how to cook their food in hot water springs.

9. The Lapps of northern Sweden keep yaks to provide transport, food and skins.

10. Emeralds are used to make jewellery because of their rich red colour.

11. The alternative name for the grunting ox is the yak.

GLOSSARY

● **Acid rain** is rain polluted by chemicals released from industrial waste, car exhausts and burning fuel. It can poison trees and plants and erode the face of buildings.

● **Altitude** is the measurement of height above sea level.

● **Avalanche** is caused when heavy snow slips down a mountainside. It can damage property and injure people and animals.

● **Block mountain** is formed when a block of rock is forced up a crack, or fault, in the Earth's crust. It often has a flat surface on top, similar to a plain, called a plateau.

● **Camouflage** hides animals against their surroundings to protect them from predators, and can help them capture prey.

● **Coniferous trees** produce cones, and are evergreen. They are found mainly in the northern hemisphere.

● **Core** is the centre of the Earth. It is thought to be solid and is likely to be made of iron and nickel.

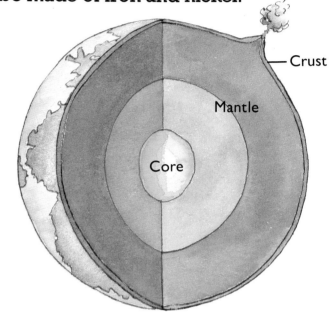

Crust

Mantle

Core

● **Crust** is the name given to the Earth's thin surface layer. Mountains are built in the crust.

● **Deciduous** trees lose all of their leaves before a cold or dry season. They cannot live in such cold climates as coniferous trees do.

● **Equator** is the imaginary line around the Earth, exactly halfway between the North and South Poles.

● **Erode** means to wear away. Mountains are eroded by the effects of wind, rain, ice and snow.

● **Evergreen** trees drop and replace their leaves throughout the year. This means that they always look green. They can grow in colder climates than deciduous trees.

● **Fold mountain** is formed when rock is crumpled and forced upwards, as the edges of two or more of the Earth's plates meet and grind together.

● **Hibernating** is how some animals survive cold weather. They fatten themselves during the warmer months, then sleep all through the long winter.

● **Latitude** is a line drawn from east to west on a map.

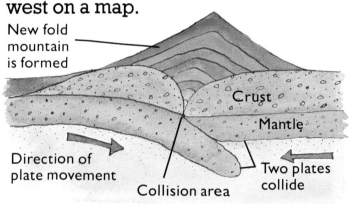

New fold mountain is formed

Crust

Mantle

Direction of plate movement

Collision area

Two plates collide

● **Mantle** is the layer of rock surrounding the Earth's core and lying beneath the crust.

● **Plate** is one of the huge slabs of rock which make up the Earth's crust.

● **Plateau** is the flat area at the top of a block mountain.

● **Pollute** means to poison air, land or water. It is often caused by the waste from human industrial activity.

● **Predator** is an animal that hunts and kills other animals for food.

● **Rain shadow** is the area on a mountainside facing away from the sea. It receives little rain. Most of the rain falls over the seaward side of the mountain.

● **Snowline** is the level on the side of a mountain above which no plant life can grow. Snow often covers the mountain above this level all the year round.

● **Treeline** is the level on a mountainside above which the climate is too cold and windy for trees to grow.

● **Volcano** is an opening in the Earth's crust from which very hot, molten rock and gas may leak and cover the surrounding land.

INDEX